WALKING CL

HERTFORD

and the LEE VALLEY

Number Forty Three in the popular series of walking guides

Contents

Walk		Miles	Page No
1	Elbow Lane	$7^1/_4$	4
2	New River	8	6
3	Sally Rainbow's Dell	6	8
4	Bengeo Lammas Land	$6^1/_2$	10
5	Dobb's Weir	7	12
6	Chelsing Tributary	$5^3/_4$	14
7	Stanstead Lock	5	16
8	Queen Hoo	$3^3/_4$	18
9	Bury Lane	3	18
10	Barwick Ford	$5^3/_4$	20
11	Stratton's Folly	$8^1/_2$	22

Walked, Written and Drawn by Clive Brown
© Clive Brown 2008 – 2015

Published by Clive Brown
ISBN 978-1-907669-43-9

PLEASE
Take care of the countryside
Your leisure is someone's livelihood

Close gates
Start no fires
Keep away from livestock and animals
Do not stray from marked paths
Take litter home
Do not damage walls, hedgerows or fences
Cross only at stiles or gates
Protect plants, trees and wildlife
Keep dogs on leads
Respect crops, machinery and rural property
Do not contaminate water

Although not essential we recommend good walking boots; during hot weather take something to drink on the way. All walks can easily be negotiated by an averagely fit person. The routes have been recently walked and surveyed, changes can however occur, please follow any signed diversions. Some paths cross fields which are under cultivation. All distances and times are approximate.

The maps give an accurate portrayal of the area, but scale has however been sacrificed in some cases for the sake of clarity and to fit restrictions of page size.

Walking Close To have taken every care in the research and production of this guide but cannot be held responsible for the safety of anyone using them.

During very wet weather, parts of these walks may become impassable through flooding, check before starting out. Stiles and rights of way can get overgrown during the summer; folding secateurs are a useful addition to a walker's rucksack.

Thanks to Angela for help in production of these booklets

Views or comments?
walkingcloseto@yahoo.co.uk

Reproduced from Ordnance Survey Mapping on behalf of The Controller of Her Majesty's Stationery Office.   © Crown Copyright License No. 100037980.

43:B

Walking Close to Hertford and the Lee Valley

It is likely that there has been a settlement at Hertford since prehistoric times. The obvious origin of the name, that here was a shallow river crossing used by deer, would have attracted human habitation. Written history starts with the synod of Hertford called by Theodore, the Archbishop of Canterbury, in 673AD. This meeting led to the establishment of a unified Christian church in England following the Roman Pattern. During the late 9th century the Danish leader Guthrum used the River Lee to get his forces into the interior of the country. His opponent King Alfred built a weir at Hertford to restrict this activity. The river was the effective boundary between Saxon Wessex and the Danes through the troubled peace of the Danelaw. Alfred's son, Edward the Elder, made the weir into a permanent feature, fortified the town and created Hertfordshire from the territory reconquered from the Danes.

Throughout the Middle Ages London took a huge amount of drinking water from the River Lee. With increasing industrial use the river started to get very polluted during Tudor times. A plan was put forward to cut a channel from Hertfordshire into central London to supply fresh clean water from the river while avoiding the pollution. The New River was constructed in 1609 by Sir Hugh Myddleton but he faced opposition from vested interests such as mill owners. This faded away when King James I agreed to pay half the construction costs (in return for half the profit). The watercourse starts at the New Gauge House (walk no 2) between Hertford and Ware, the route keeps close to the river to Rye House near Hoddesdon and then veers off to the west. It originally ran on the surface to Clerkenwell; in modern times alterations have been made and much of the river now flows underground to Stoke Newington.

The source of the River Lee is in Leagrave Park in Luton. It flows south and east, past Harpenden and Welwyn Garden City to Hertford where it is joined by the rivers Beane, Rib and Mimram. From Hertford Castle Weir the river has been canalised as the Lee Valley Navigation and heads south to join the River Thames at Leamouth just east of the Isle of Dogs. The Lee was the subject of a series of Acts of Parliament between the 15th century and the late Victorian era to cope with ever increasing river traffic. The course of the river was straightened and a series of locks installed to improve navigation. Commercial traffic continued until the 1980s; now the river is even busier with leisure boating and other water based activities.

We feel that it would be difficult to get lost with the instructions and maps in this booklet, but please take care it is obviously much easier to get lost in trees than in open countryside. We recommend carrying an Ordnance Survey map, the walks are on Explorer Map Nos 174,182 and 194; Landranger Nos. 166 and 167 cover at a smaller scale. Roads, geographical features and buildings, not on our map but visible from the walk can be easily identified.

1   Elbow Lane

$7^{1}/_{4}$ Miles $3^{1}/_{2}$ Hours

Find a parking space in Hertford Heath, shop and pubs but no other facilities. Start from the 'Silver Fox' pub on London Road.

1   Head north on London Road with the open fields to the left, for 250yds to the signpost on the left. Turn left through the kissing gate and go down the right hand field edge with the hedge to the right. Continue past the marker post, through the wide gap and over the field ahead, this field may be under cultivation but a path should be visible within any crop.

2   Bear left at the trees and right at the signpost, with Great Stock Wood to the right. Cross the footbridge, bear left across (a track should be visible) the corner of the field and along the edge of Little Stock Wood. Go through the gap at the end and bear right over the field (a path is normally well marked) up to the farm road. Follow this road left and continue between hedges over the stile and on to the road.

3   Turn left/ahead and carry on to the byway signpost on the right, (just before Blackfields Farm); turn right along this hedged track. Turn right at the junction, then immediate left back to the original direction. Carry on all the way to the road and turn left for 220yds to the signpost.

4   Go through the narrow gate and up to the four way signpost. Turn right, signposted Pembridge Lane, along the wide footpath between hedges and go through the metal kissing gate. Keep direction on the right hand edge of the next two fields.

5   Continue through the gate at the edge of the trees and bear left on the obvious path through Cowheath Wood. Bear right and keep ahead at the cross roads to the marker post at a fork in the path, carry on for 120yds and follow the path left. At the marker post turn right downslope, cross the footbridge and turn left up the opposite slope. Bear right at the fork in the track and go through the kissing gate to the more substantial path and bear left/ahead to a gravel driveway.

6   Turn left with the low wooden posts to the left; as the driveway turns left keep ahead downslope on the narrower track between trees. Turn right at the bottom of the slope through the kissing gate at the Danemead information board, walk along the boardwalk and path with the stream to the left.

7   At the wider substantial road, take the footpath left of the ford and continue along Elbow Lane, the course of Roman Ermine Street, over the minor road at Goose Green for a mile and a half to the corner of London Road in Hertford Heath.

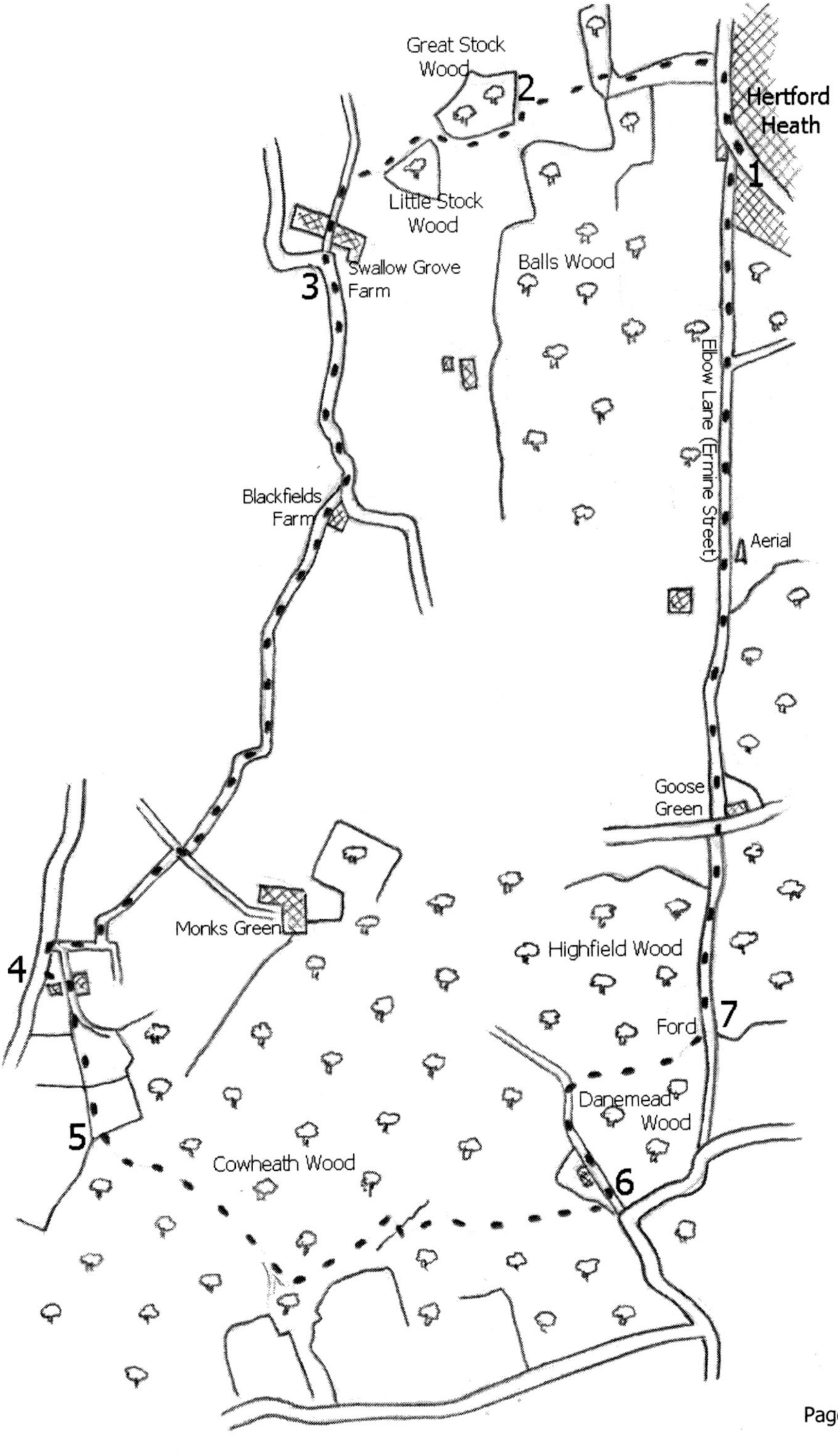

Great Stock Wood
2
Hertford Heath
1
Little Stock Wood
Swallow Grove Farm
3
Balls Wood
Elbow Lane (Ermine Street)
Blackfields Farm
Aerial
Goose Green
Monks Green
4
Highfield Wood
7
Ford
Danemead Wood
5
Cowheath Wood
6

2   New River

8 Miles $3^3/_4$ Hours

Park in the Hartham Common car park off Bengeo Street/Port Hill in Hertford, (pay and display). Toilets close, all other facilities in the town.

1 Go back out of the car park entrance and turn right up the slope for 120yds to the ornate gates of Warren Meadows Lodge, turn right and follow the wide tarmac path through the trees. Continue ahead into the cemetery and bear left through the gate at the back of the church. Take the tarmac path right between the wall and the wrought iron fence and turn left through the kissing gate.

2 Walk down to the river by the footbridge at the bottom right; turn sharp left with the fence to the right and cross the metal and concrete footbridge/stile ahead. Bear right to the opposite corner and go over the more substantial footbridge, take the road right across the bridge and turn immediate right at the signpost.

3 Bear left between trees and keep ahead on the black arrowed RUPP, continue between fences and ahead across fields. Carry on along the field edge with the fence to the left, turn left through the gate and right back to the original direction along the potholed hardcore road. Just before the bridge turn right downslope with the A10 to the left, down to the River Lee.

4 Turn left and go under the A10, go off to the left and carry on with the sports ground to the left. In the corner follow the path left and turn right across the footbridge over the Lee, turn left with the river now left. Keep direction over the road by the bridge at Ware all the way to Hardmead Lock.

5 Turn right, through the bushes and over the railway, go up to the New River and turn right, along the path with the river to the left. At the road junction continue ahead with the river now right to the junction at the level crossing. Go through the kissing gate along the path with the New River again on the left; follow the path as it turns left and cross back over the river near the white hut.

6 Keep on the left bank of the river over the railway and under the A10, turning right, to the brick building (New Gauge House) where the New River starts. Turn left along the tarmac path with the River Lee to the right; continue past Hertford Lock and the factories on the left.

7 Cross over the bridge at the black three way signpost and bear immediate left over the black and white footbridge. Go down the steps to the right and bear left below the weir. Turn left between the weir and the canoe club, keep direction ahead back to the car park and your vehicle.

Page Six

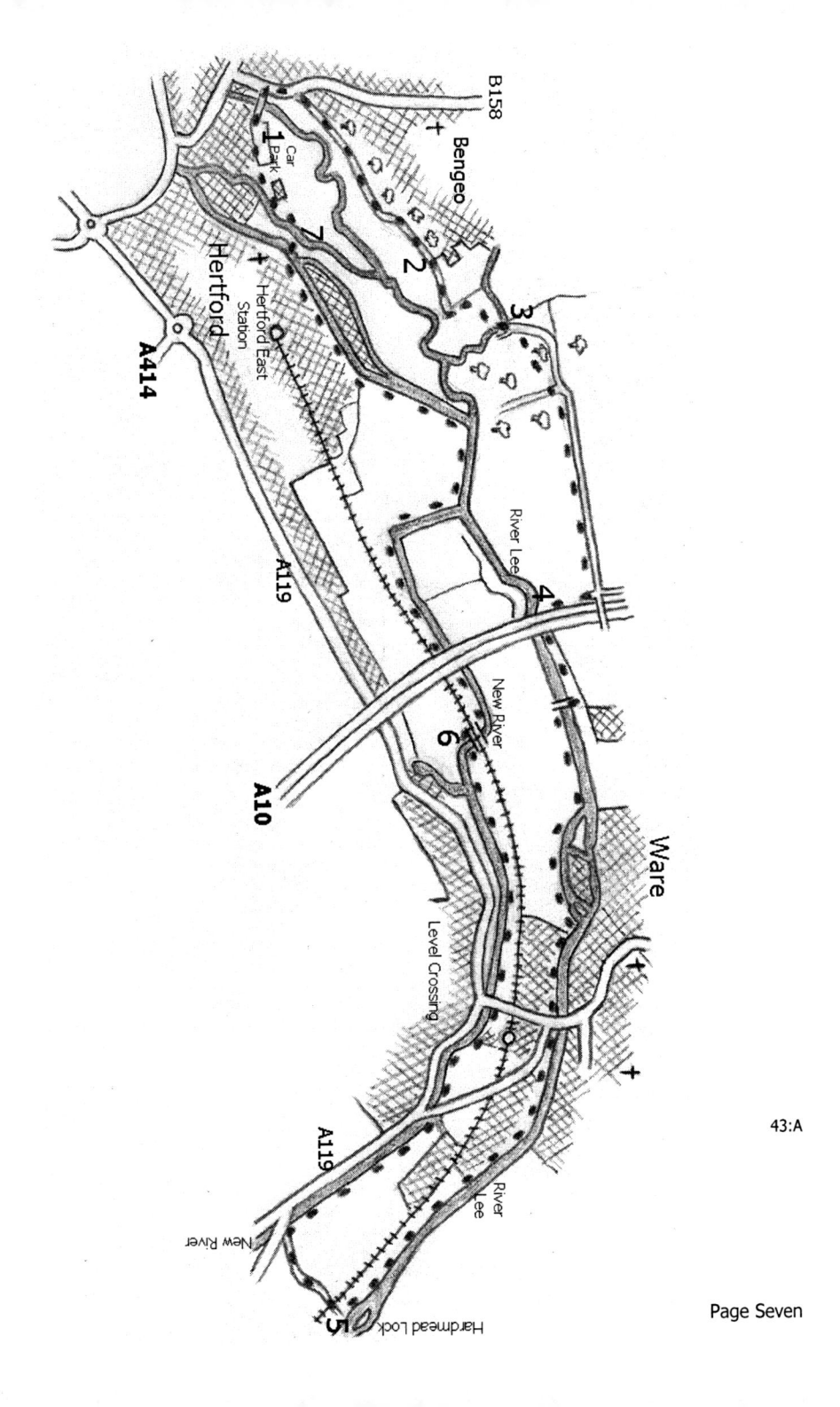

43:A

Page Seven

3   Sally Rainbow's Dell

6 Miles   3 Hours

Use the car park next to the village hall and playing field, west of the High Street in Watton at Stone. Toilets at the building; post office, shops and pubs in the village.

1 Facing away from the car park take the path to the left, up a slight slope through barriers to the school turn right and immediate left at the signpost along the path between the hedge and the wall. As the hedge ends turn left, keep ahead to the road and turn right across the bridge over the railway.

2 Carry on ahead past the cul-de-sac sign to the farm and bear left with the second pond to the right. Keep ahead through a gate, past a marker post and continue through the trees to the junction of paths.

3 Turn right, past the farm buildings along the farm road with the trees to the right, past the open fields to the marker post 90yds after the trees start again. Take the right hand fork through the trees; at the junction keep ahead past the metal barrier to the crossroads of tracks.

4 Turn left, still through trees, on a narrower hardcore path; keep direction bearing right through a dip and keep right. At a marker post close to the far side of the wood, bear left down a sunken path for 85yds to a marker post; follow the path left past Sally Rainbow's Dell and continue along this hedge lined path to the road.

5 Take the road left for a third of a mile; as the road swings left go straight on past the bridleway signpost along the gravelly farm track with the trees to the left. At the marker post, turn left and immediate right, with the trees to the left. Take a diagonal across this field, which may be under cultivation although a path should be well marked, to the far corner. Go through the hedge gap and keep direction over this field to the hedge gap.

6 Bear left on the field edge with the small wood to the left, up to the marker post and turn right along the right hand field edge with the hedge to the right. Turn left at the trees and follow the edge of the wood to the right. Bear right at the marker post, down the fenced path and under the railway, keep on this path to the A119 in Stapleford. Turn left along the roadside path to Gobions Lane.

7 Go through the gate at the signpost opposite and cross the field ahead to the farm. Step over the stile and walk past the front of the house, turn left on the path between the hedge and the fence. At the top turn right, through the gap and carry on across the field, (a track should be visible); continue direction into the dip, over the footbridge and up the other side. Go through the trees and keep direction ahead, through the gap up the left hand edge of the right hand field.

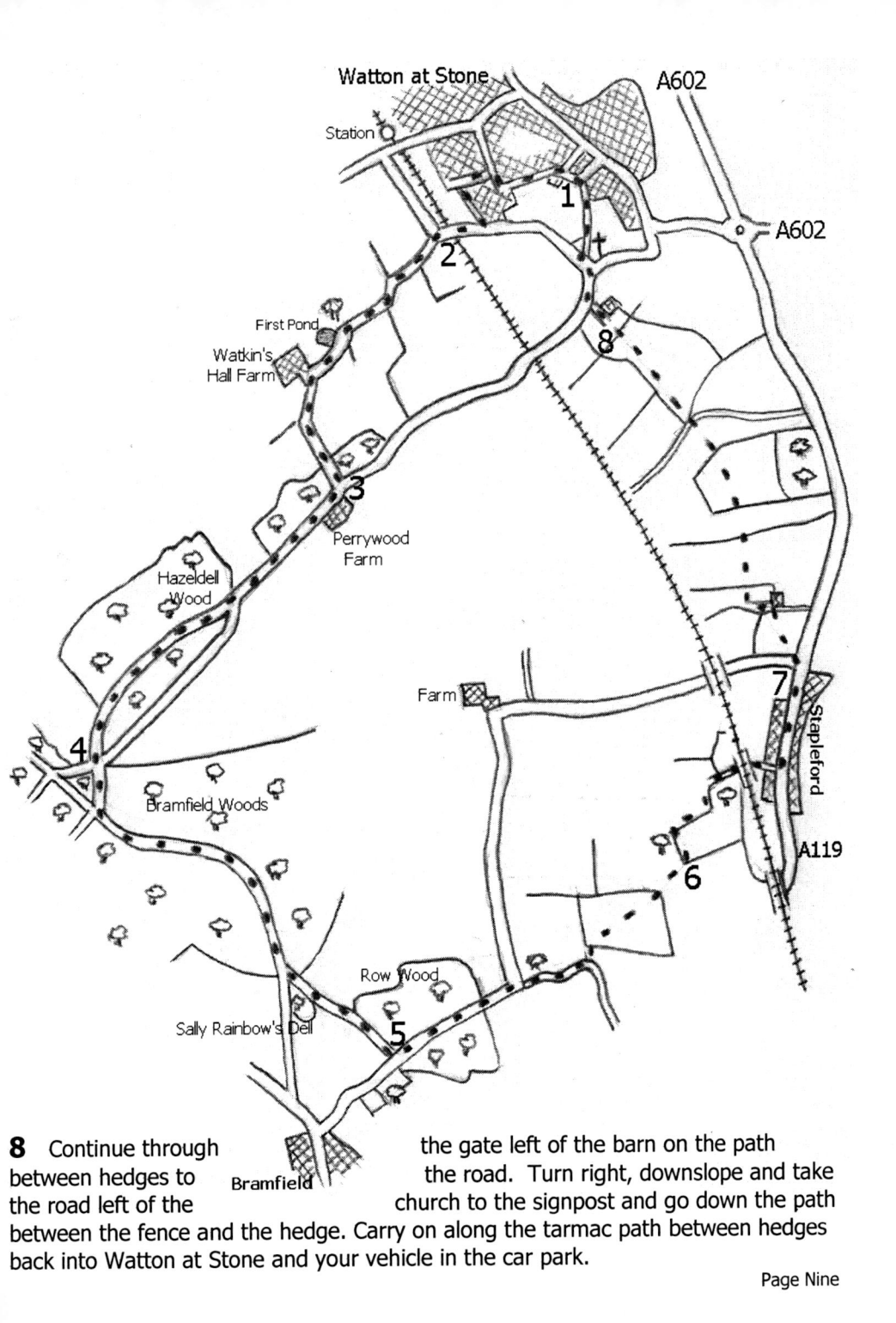

8 Continue through the gate left of the barn on the path between hedges to the road. Turn right, downslope and take the road left of the church to the signpost and go down the path between the fence and the hedge. Carry on along the tarmac path between hedges back into Watton at Stone and your vehicle in the car park.

Page Nine

4   Bengeo Lammas Land

6½ Miles   3 Hours

Find a parking space in Tonwell. Pub the 'Robin Hood and Little John' but no other facilities.

1   Go up Temple Lane and keep ahead along the hardcore farm road to Bengeo Temple Farm. Bear left on the track with the hedge to the right and walk up to the far corner, step over the stile and follow the concrete road to the marker post.
2   Turn left along the tarmac road to the A602 and cross this very busy road extremely carefully. Take the minor road to the right and follow the road left over the junction to the signpost on the right. Turn right down the left hand field edge through the trees and over the driveway; continue direction with the wall to the left.
3   Climb over the ladder stile to the left and keep ahead past the marker post, over the stile and on to the driveway. Bear left at the angled crossroads and walk up to the cattle grid. Turn left over the bridge, bear right over the second bridge and bear right through the kissing gate in the metal rail fence ahead.
4   Turn left along the track parallel to the River Beane, go over the ladder stile and continue between the fence and the trees with the river to the right. Join the tarmac road to the junction in Stapleford and turn right, take the drive left through the church gateway and bear right on the footpath right of the church. Keep on the path and bear left upslope to the farm road, turn right to the corner at Bullsmill.
5   Take the narrow tarmac road left between shoulder high banks up to the junction, turn right for 75yds and go to the left at the byway signpost along the track past the right hand edge of Bardon Clumps. Bear left at the signpost at the disused quarry, past the right hand edge of the trees and keep ahead across the open ground. Join the more substantial track to the left, through the trees with Bengeo Lammas Land to the right.
6   Keep direction on the road through Chapmore End, bear right at the top of the duck pond to the signpost and bear left on the track along the field edge with the hedge to the left. Carry on over the wooden footbridge, up the grassy slope and cross (carefully) back over the busy A602 into Tonwell to find your vehicle.

The prominent water tower at Tonwell was built in 1964 and it holds 50,000 gallons of water. Its striking design contrasts sharply with the 1930s water tower in nearby Bengeo. The name Bengeo is a derivative of 'ridge above the River Beane'.

43:A

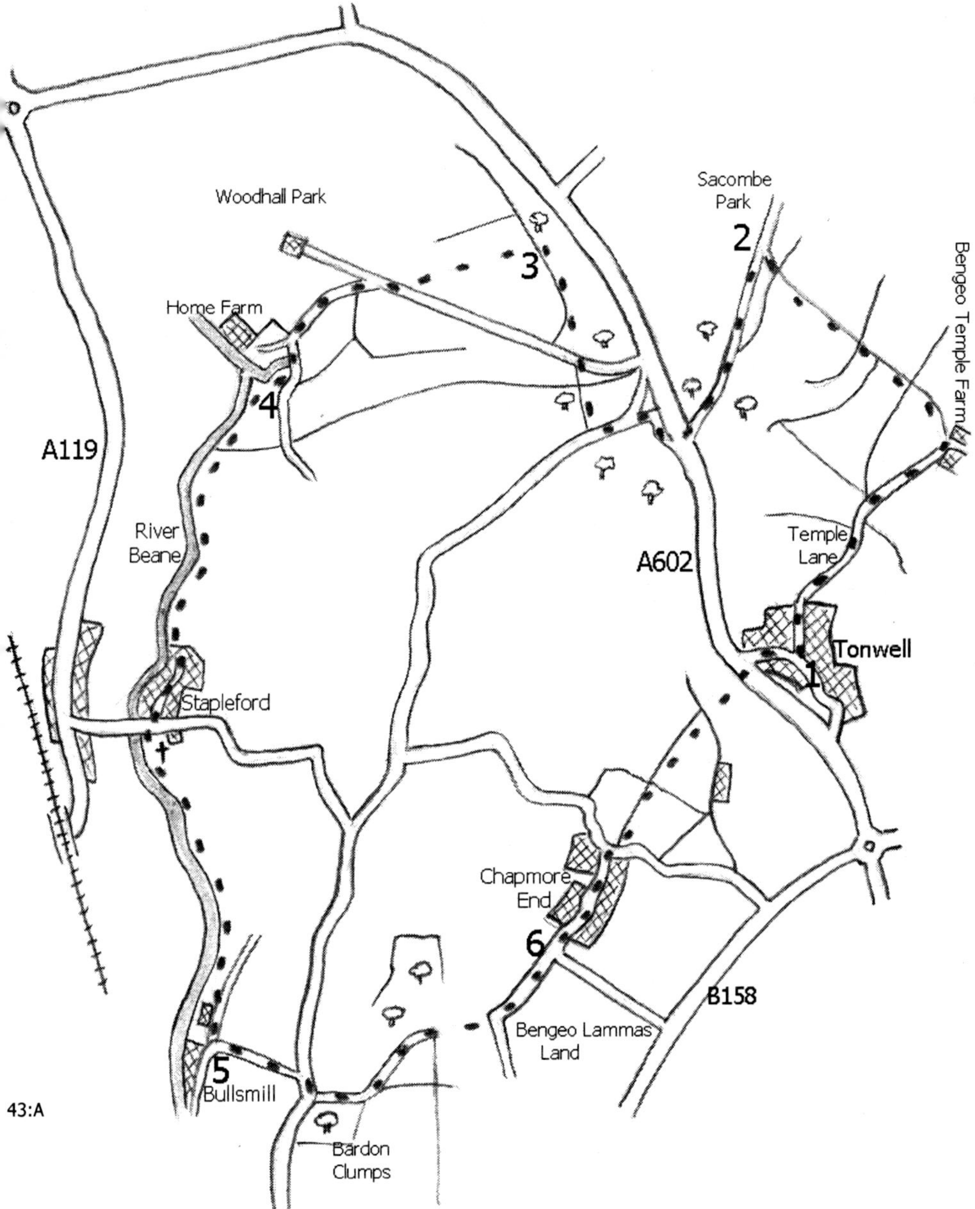
Woodhall Park
Sacombe Park
2
3
Bengeo Temple Farm
Home Farm
4
A119
River Beane
A602
Temple Lane
Tonwell
1
Stapleford
Chapmore End
6
B158
Bengeo Lammas Land
5
Bullsmill
Bardon Clumps

43:A

5   Dobb's Weir

7 Miles   3$^1/_2$ Hours

Use the car park at Dobb's Weir, next to the River Lee in Hoddesdon. Toilets on site, café/shop adjacent and pub the 'Fish and Eels' across the road.

1   Go back to the road and cross the narrow bridge over the river. Turn right with the railings and the river to the right. Keep ahead over the footbridge right of the weir and turn right along the towpath with the river still right. Carry on all the way to the lock at Feilde's Weir.

2   Turn right over the footbridge past the lock-keeper's cottage and turn left up to the weir. Cross the footbridge ahead and turn right along the signposted towpath Stort Navigation, keeping the river to the left. Walk past Lower Lock to the marker post as the navigation swings left, turn right then almost immediate left in the corner up to the marker post in the inset corner to the right.

3   Take the field edge uphill; (the path goes right over the footbridge and runs up the other side of the hedge, but it is often easier to keep the hedge on the right), to the top corner. Turn right through the wide gap and left along the field edge in the original direction with the concrete fence to the left. Cross the stile in the corner on to the road and turn right to the stile on the left as the road drops downhill.

4   Go along the field edge to the left along the top of the slope, over the stile in the boundary and turn right in the corner. Walk downslope and turn almost immediate left through the open gateway. Continue upslope now, still on the left hand field edge and follow the farm track left and right up to the top.

5   Bear right through the wide gateway and carry on along the left hand field edge with the tall hedge to the left. Go through the gap in the corner, past the marker post and through the trees, continue ahead on the edge of the narrow then the larger field. Keep ahead through the metal kissing gate, follow the enclosed path and turn right just before the chimney down the hardcore driveway to the road.

6   Turn left and carefully walk along the edge of this very busy road, keep right at the junction down to the signpost as the road swings left. Turn right down the bridleway (Tinkers Lane) and keep direction on the grass surface. Bear left over the footbridge and slight right uphill between the fence and the hedge. Carry on uphill
Completed on the next Page (Fourteen)

River Stort Navigation

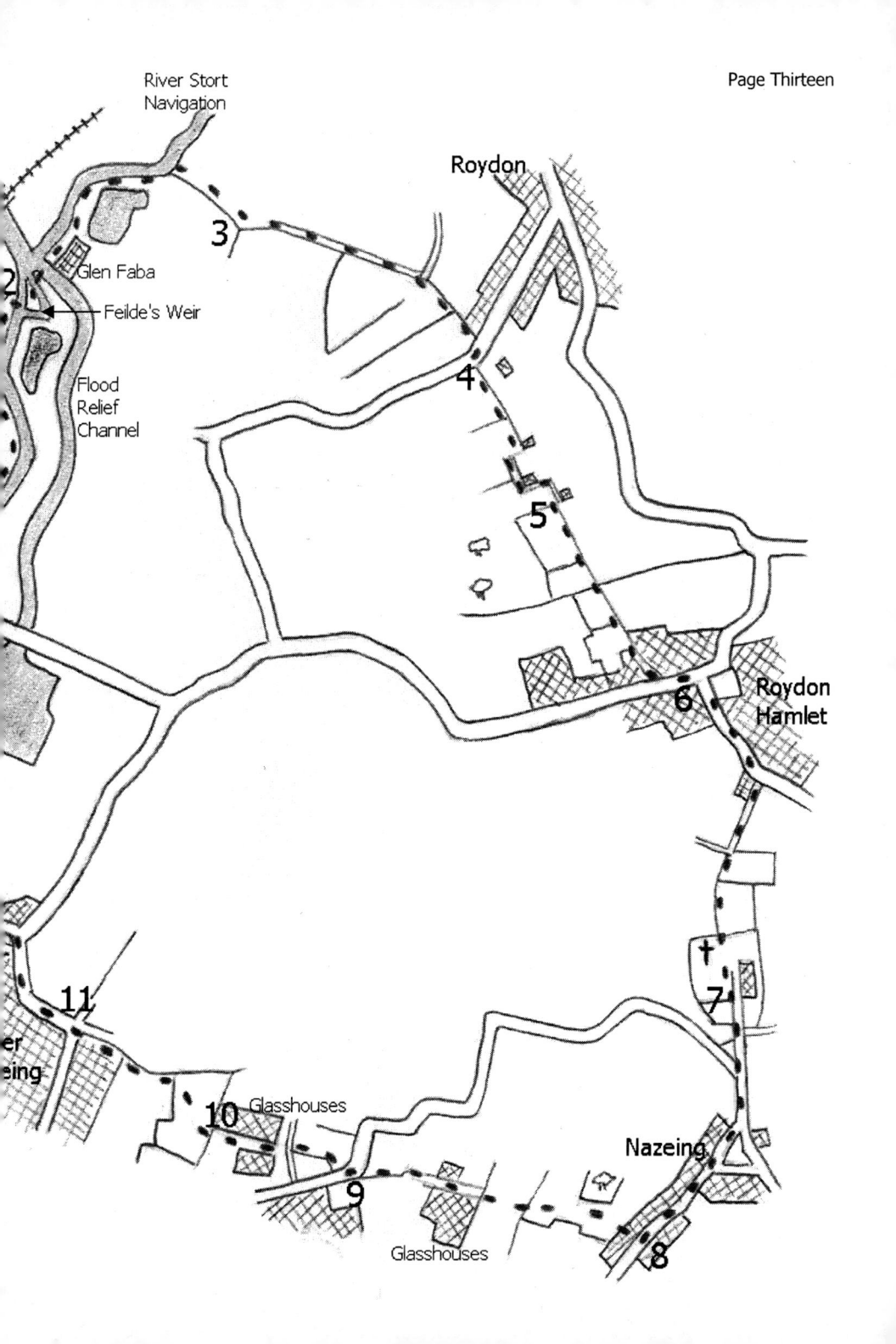

Page Thirteen

Roydon

Glen Faba

Feilde's Weir

Flood Relief Channel

Roydon Hamlet

Nazeing

Glasshouses

Glasshouses

Completion of 5 Dobb's Weir from the previous Page
through the trees and the undergrowth and follow the path through the churchyard left of the church.

7 Leave by the covered gateway and keep direction along the drive between hedges, past the first junction, up Betts Lane and turn right into Back Lane. Go through the village for 500yds to the signpost opposite Park Cottage and turn right up the narrow hedged path.

8 Bear left and step over the stile, continue downhill over the solitary stile and bear left to the left hand field edge. Go over the stile and keep ahead through the field of low shrubs; cross the footbridge and carry on with the glasshouses to the left. Bear left and cross a footbridge to the right, continue the original direction with the hedge to the right, through a wide path and along the left hand field edge to the road at a corner.

9 Cross to the signpost, go through the gap and bear right over the field to the stile near the far corner. Keep direction over the road and the stile opposite, bear right over the footbridge and carry on along the dyke edge with the conifers to the right. Continue with a glasshouse again on the right, carry on ahead through the trees and uphill on the left hand field edge with the hedge to the left.

10 At the top bear right down to the bottom corner, go through the gap and keep ahead on the field edge with the trees to the right. Step over the stile and continue between the metal railings and the hedge up to the road.

11 Carry on right/ahead along this busy road, follow it right and then left at the junction along Meadgate Road. Keep direction all the way to the river, turn right on the wide track along the bank and continue to the car park at Dobb's Weir and your vehicle.

6   Chelsing Tributary

$5^3/_4$ Miles $2^3/_4$ Hours

Find a parking space in Tonwell. Pub the 'Robin Hood and Little John' but no other facilities.

1 Walk back out of the village to the junction with the A602, cross at the refuge on the right hand (Stevenage) side and continue through the hedge gap at the signpost. Turn immediate left, signposted to Chapmore End, up to the hedge gap and turn right down the sloping field and across the footbridge. Continue direction up the hill with the hedge to the right, up to the road at Chapmore End.

2 Follow the road left down to the B158 and cross this surprisingly busy road carefully. Carry on bearing slight left with the hedge to the right, go through the boundary at the hedge gap and turn left at the corner by the A602. Turn right through the subway and right back up to the River Rib, take the field edge up to the old road and turn right.

3 At the dead end turn left at the signpost along the hardcore driveway and keep ahead on the wide path through the trees. Bear right after just over half a mile and left at the marker post between houses. Turn almost immediate left at the signpost for Thundridge down the slope to the marker post and take the path right. Follow the marker posts along the edge of the trees, through the boundary and continue with the trees still right.

4 At the road turn left and back over the Rib to the 'Anchor', turn left for 220yds to the footpath signpost. Take the driveway right, signposted Sacombe and keep direction upslope past the marker post. Continue straight on through the trees and carry on ahead between fields, bear left through the hedge gap at the boundary keeping the hedge to the right and then Furzeground Wood to the left.

Completed on the next Page (Sixteen)

Page Fifteen

Completion of 6 Chelsing Tributary from the previous Page

5 Turn left at the far corner with the trees still left and continue direction with the ground on the left sloping down to Chelsing Tributary. Bear left into the trees and turn right at the junction, up to the marker post. Cross the footbridge, go through the kissing gate and walk past the buildings of Bengeo Temple Farm.

6 Go left through this next kissing gate and carry on ahead on the hardcore farm road. Continue past the water tower, into Tonwell along Temple Lane to find your vehicle.

---

7 Stanstead Lock

5 Miles $2^{1}/_{2}$ Hours

Use the car park off the High Street in Stanstead Abbotts, most facilities locally but no toilets.

1 Leave the car park to the left, walk up to the mini-roundabout and turn left to Abbotts Way and take this road uphill. At the top, go slight left, climb up the two sets of steps and bear left for 20yds; turn right past the barrier up the slope between the houses.

2 Continue ahead slight left over the field which may be under cultivation although a path should be well marked and go past the marker post. At the signpost bear left parallel with the telegraph poles, towards Little Briggens along the road between the houses. Turn left at the marker post, between the barns and up the hardcore farm track to the crossroads.

3 Follow this track past the left hand side of Young Wood, keep left as the trees end and go down the slope to the old railway line.

4 Turn left across the bridge over the River Ash up to the end and turn left over the footbridge next to the ford. Go up the slope to the junction, turn right past the house and step over the stile ahead. Follow the field edge with the fence then the river to the right and cross the stile back on to the old railway line.

5 Take the track left between the trees and cross back over the Ash on the footbridge. Continue on the old railway track under the bridge and through the kissing gate into Lee Valley Park. Bear left to the Lee Valley Navigation and cross over the footbridge.

6 Descend to the towpath and follow the path south with the river to the left. Carry on along the path, past Stanstead Lock to the road bridge at Stanstead Abbotts and turn left along the High Street to the car park and your vehicle.

43:A

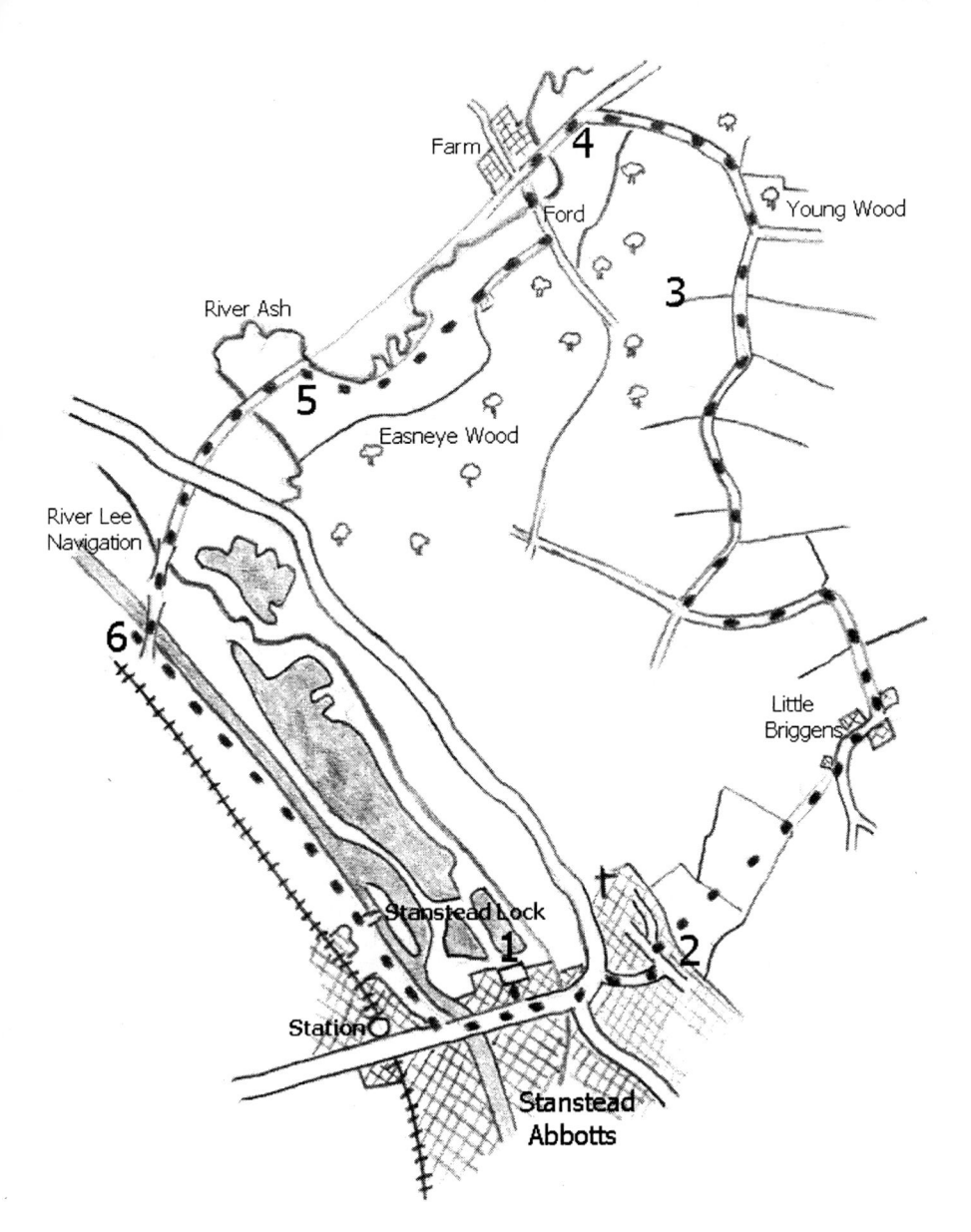

The River Ash joins the Lee close to Stanstead Lock and a little further on the River Stort also links up at Feilde's Weir (walk no 5). Most of the Stort had been canalised into the Stort Navigation at about the same time as the Lee. After a less successful history it was acquired in 1911 by the River Lee Navigation for the nominal sum of five shillings (25 pence).

43:A

Page Seventeen

8   Queen Hoo

$3^3/_4$ Miles   2 Hours

Use the car park at the playing field on Bury Lane in Bramfield village. No toilets; shop/post office and pub the 'Grandison Arms'.

1 Turn right from the car park entrance, back to Main Road and turn left along the roadside path out of the village up to the bridleway signpost to Datchworth. Turn right past the tall metal bollards along this wide path, bearing left to a marker post at a crossroads of tracks.
2 Take the substantial track to the left for 280yds and follow as it turns to the right up to a T-junction. Turn left, walk down to the road and take the road right for 325yds to the junction with Tewin Hill.
3 Turn left along the road to the signpost at Queen Hoo and take the track left towards Tewin. Follow this track between fields then trees to the marker post where the trees end on the left.
4 Turn left on this path along the field edge with the trees to the left into the corner. Turn right and follow the path on the field edge around to the potholed driveway (the path cuts the last corner across the field close to the gate).
5 Take the driveway right, back to the parking area and your vehicle.

9   Bury Lane

3 Miles $1^1/_2$ Hours

Use the car park in Bramfield village, as above.

1 Turn left from the car park entrance along the rutted bridleway Bury Lane to the gates at Bramfieldbury. Turn left across the corner of the field to the right, this field may be under cultivation but a track should be well marked within any crop.
2 Carry on around the edge of the field with the tall hedge and then the lower hedge to the right, into the corner. Turn left with the trees to the right, up to the marker post at the corner.
3 Walk down the dirt farm road to the left between fields to a junction and take the narrower path straight on, past a marker post through an archway in the hedge and continue ahead between the buildings of Bacon's Farm.

1 Queen Hoo
1 Bury Lane

Map labels: To Datchworth, Bramfield Woods, Queen Hoo, Row Wood, Sally Rainbow's Dell, Bramfield, To Hertford, Bury Lane, Bramfield Park Wood, Ruin, Westend House, Bacon's Farm

The same map is used for walks 8 and 9 which may easily be combined into a total length of 6 miles

4 Bear left along the potholed farm driveway to the road and turn left for 380yds to the footpath signpost.   Take the path left, signposted Bramfield village, with Westend House to the right, along to the marker post. Turn right on the path past a double telegraph pole and keep on this path more or less parallel with the line of telegraph poles.

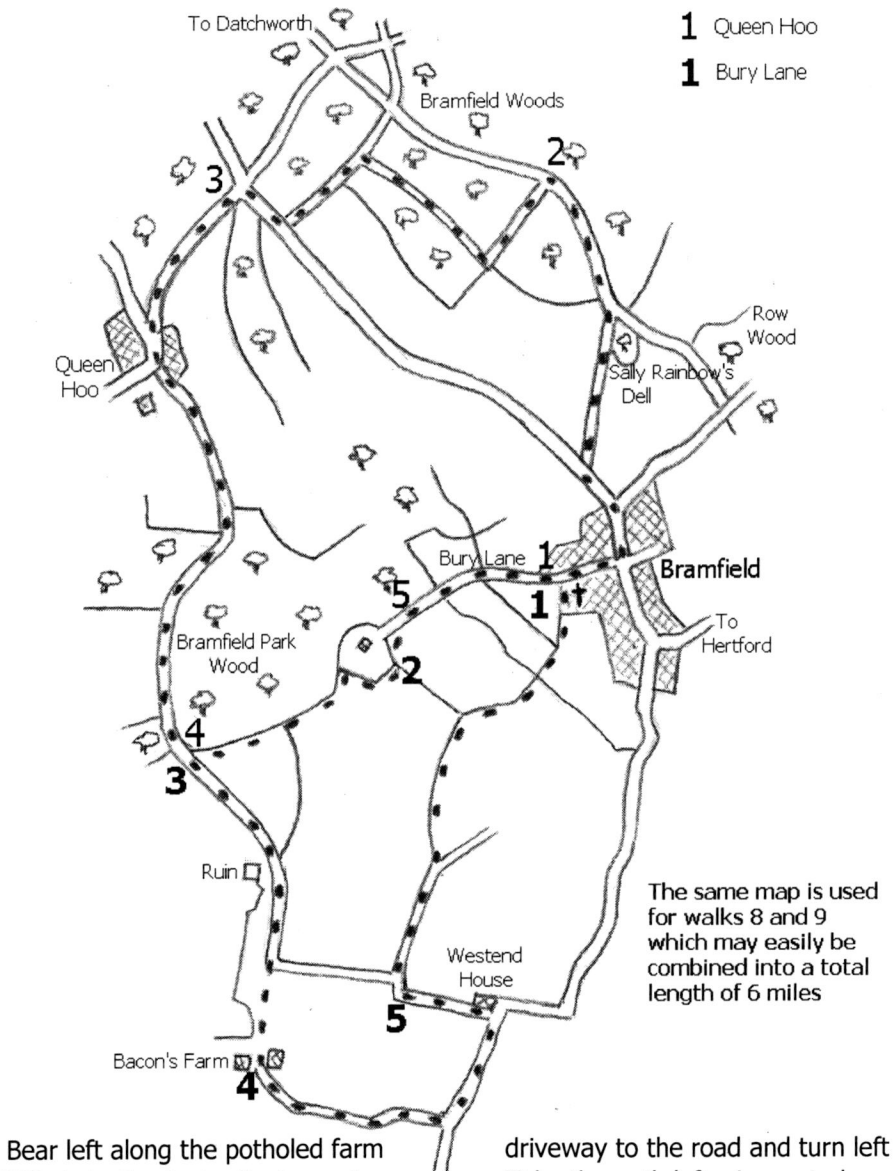

5 Turn right with a tall hedge to the left to the marker post at the end and bear left across two fields (tracks should be visible within any crops). Go through the wide hedge gap and cross the playing field to the parking area and your vehicle.

10   Barwick Ford

5¾ Miles   2½ Hours

Find a parking space in Thundridge or Wadesmill, on the old A10 north of Ware. Shop/post office but no other facilities.

1   Start from the Thundridge side of the river and go down the slope away from the main road past the post office and the phone box. Turn right, between the houses up the slope (Ermine Street) to the signpost at the top left. Take the narrow path (no 25) signposted to Thundridge Old Church; go through the kissing gate and keep direction through the next kissing gate. Continue between fields and follow the tarmac then hardcore track beneath the A10.

2   Bear right to the signpost and take the path towards Cold Christmas, with the ruined church to the left. Keep ahead over the driveway and past the marker post at the footbridge, carry on with the river to the left. At the marker post on the right hand river bend turn right between fields upslope on the track flanked by hedges. Turn right at the road down to the corner and go through the gates on the left.

3   Walk along the gravely road and bear left between the fence and the pond to the wide gap on the right. Bear left across the open field, which may be under cultivation although a path should be visible within any crop, to the thicket. Continue on the track along the right hand field edge with the trees and the bushes to the right, over the farm road to the trees at the far corner. Turn right on the track between fields to the marker post, cross the field to the left to the signpost visible in the hedge, slight left (a track should be well marked).

4   At the road continue through the farmyard ahead, right of the silos to the footpath signpost. Bear left on the narrow path between fields, past a marker post and into the trees. Keep ahead bearing left downhill to the marker post and turn right down the steeper slope to the road.

5   Turn left and go over the footbridge next to Barwick Ford, keep ahead to the gate and turn left along the farm track on the left hand field edge with the hedge to the left. At the boundary turn right up the hill along the right hand field edge, hedge now right. Continue slight right with the hedge still right, carry on between fields and then with the trees of (oblong) Round Wood to the left.

6   At the corner turn left along the hardcore farm road, bearing left past the trees of Aldeck Spring to the double metal gates. Turn right on this farm road with the farmyard and the hedge to the left to the marker post at the white gate.

7   Take the driveway to the left and fork immediate right towards Youngsbury. Bear right over the cattle grid and follow this road through parkland to the A10.

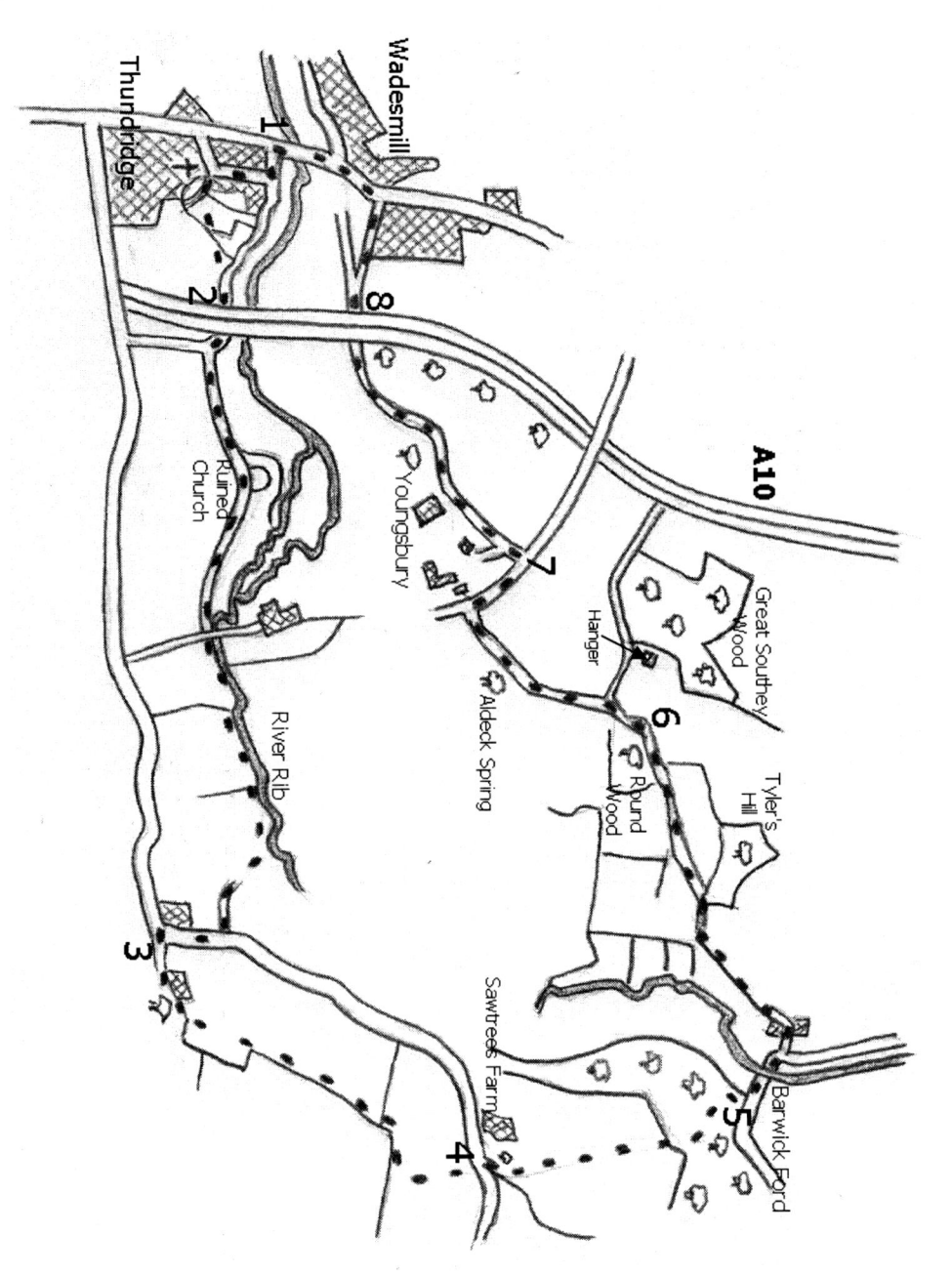

8 Keep ahead beneath the road and fork right at the marker post, go through the gate and continue along the road into Wadesmill and the old A10, to find your vehicle.

Page Twenty One

11 Stratton's Folly

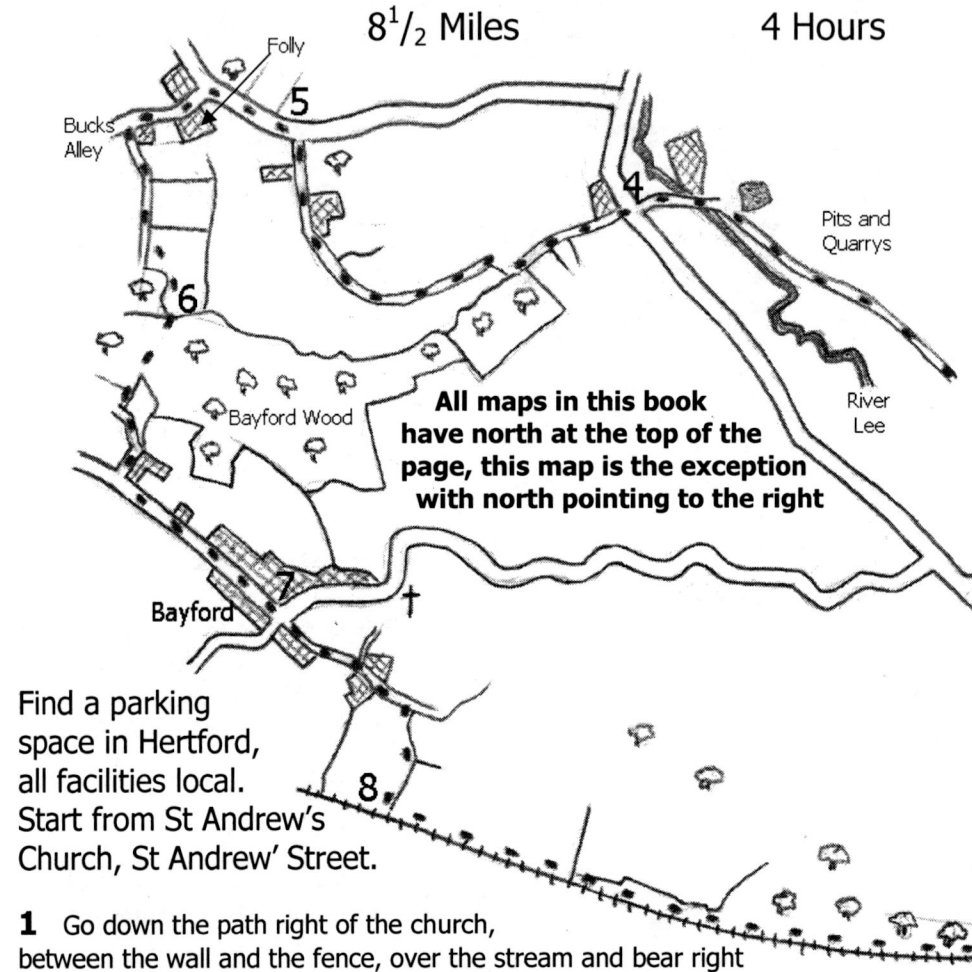

8½ Miles   4 Hours

Map labels: Folly, Bucks Alley, 5, 4, Pits and Quarrys, 6, Bayford Wood, River Lee, Bayford, 7, 8

All maps in this book have north at the top of the page, this map is the exception with north pointing to the right

Find a parking space in Hertford, all facilities local. Start from St Andrew's Church, St Andrew' Street.

1 Go down the path right of the church, between the wall and the fence, over the stream and bear right with the stream to the right. Carry on with the road to the right and turn right over the dual carriageway at Evron crossing. Turn right along the pavement and immediate left into West Street. After 150yds at the footpath signpost, take the path left between walls; follow this path right, along the backs of the houses and go down the steps to the road.

2 Continue ahead on the tarmac track, past the sports ground and carry on under the railway bridge. Keep ahead on the wide path as it goes through a fence gap and turn left at the cycleway signpost and along the old railway track. Carry on for

43:A

Page Twenty Two

two thirds of a mile past the old station to the marker post and turn left down the stepped path to the road.

3 Turn left for 120yds to the signpost and take the bridleway right, past the barrier up the wide track between the fence and the hedge. Go around the dogleg at the junction; continue between fences through the industrial area and cross over the River Lee to the road.

4 Cross and carry on ahead past the signpost up the wide path between hedges. At the marker post bear right alongside the dry stream bed and the high and dry footbridge. Continue up the slope and keep on this track past the house; go along the gravel then tarmac topped driveway to the end of Stockings Lane.

5 Turn left, walk up the road past Stratton's Folly to the junction and turn left into Bucks Alley. After 180yds turn left over the stile down the wide enclosed path and over the next stile; step over the final stile ahead by the fence and bear left across the field, a track should be seen in the grass. Keep direction past the gate and over the next field to the signpost at the trees.

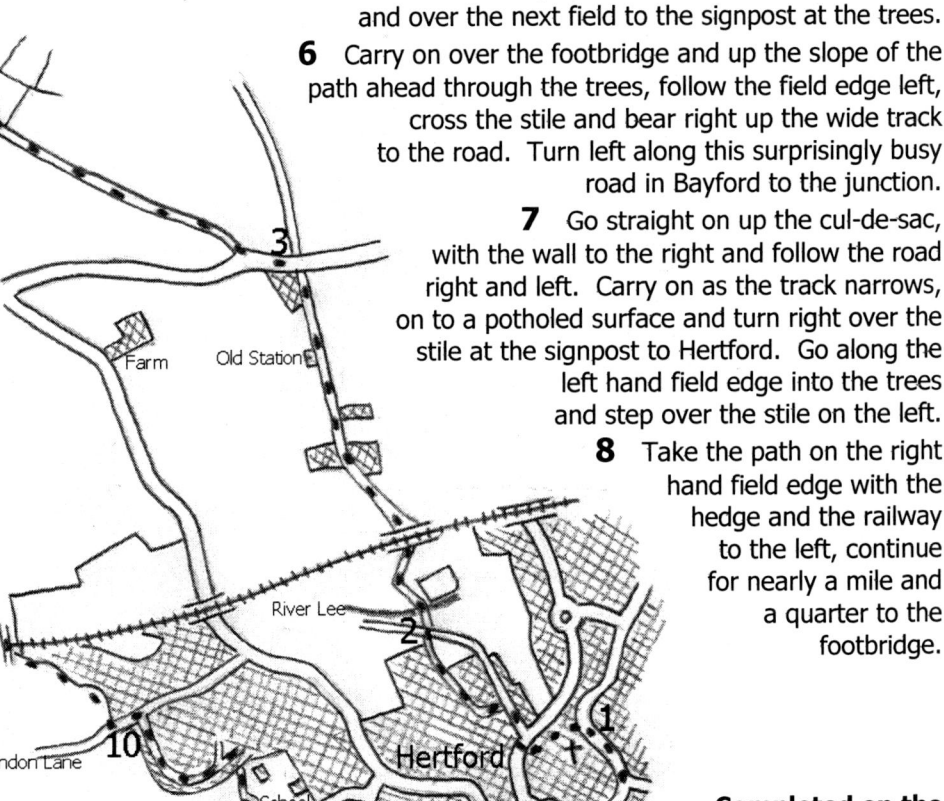

6 Carry on over the footbridge and up the slope of the path ahead through the trees, follow the field edge left, cross the stile and bear right up the wide track to the road. Turn left along this surprisingly busy road in Bayford to the junction.

7 Go straight on up the cul-de-sac, with the wall to the right and follow the road right and left. Carry on as the track narrows, on to a potholed surface and turn right over the stile at the signpost to Hertford. Go along the left hand field edge into the trees and step over the stile on the left.

8 Take the path on the right hand field edge with the hedge and the railway to the left, continue for nearly a mile and a quarter to the footbridge.

Completed on the next Page (Twenty Four)

Page Twenty Three

Completion of 11 Strattons Folly from the previous Page

9 Turn right over the railway and bear left along the field edge away from the railway with the hedge to the left, through the boundary and on to the road through the corner at the bottom left.

10 Turn left and immediate right into Mandeville Road, carry on uphill to Wilton Crescent and turn right. Turn right at the signpost and keep ahead past the signpost on the right, along the enclosed path between hedges to the road.

11 Bear left down Queens Road and continue down to the main road in Hertford, cross via the subway, back into the town centre to find your vehicle.

The Folly was built in 1789 by John Stratton so that he could keep watch on ships sailing on the Thames (15 miles away!). It is built on an octagonal base, has four storeys and is 100ft high. It is a now a private house.

The Walking Close to series in Eastern England

The Norfolk Broads (Northern Area)	Newmarket
Epping Forest	Lavenham
The Colne near Colchester	Dedham Vale
The Cam and the Granta near Cambridge	Grafham Water
The Orwell near Ipswich	Thetford Forest
Clare, Cavendish and Haverhill	Stowmarket
The Stour near Sudbury	Woburn Abbey
The Norfolk Broads (Southern Area)	Huntingdonshire
The Nene near Peterborough	The Isle of Ely
North West Norfolk (Hunstanton and Wells)	Aldeburgh, Snape
North Norfolk (Cromer and Sheringham)	and Thorpeness
Southwold and the Suffolk Coast	

Also by Clive Brown:-

'Easy Walking in South Bedfordshire and the North Chilterns'

Published by the Book Castle @ £8-99
37 walks in your favourite style

e-mail: walkingcloseto@yahoo.co.uk for the best price

43:B

Page Twenty Four